MOJO

Programming language for all of AI

Author Name: Badal Tripathy

Manual Version: 1.0

May 15, 2023

DISCLAIMER

© NPZEN.com
All Rights Reserved

http://www.npzen.com/
Email: NPZENAF@GMAIL.COM

TABLE OF CONTENTS

- **Chapter 1: Introducing Mojo**
  - What is Mojo and why is it unique?
  - A brief history of Mojo and its origins
  - Understanding the design philosophy behind Mojo
  - Installing and setting up the Mojo development environment

- **Chapter 2: Getting Started with Mojo**
  - The basics of Mojo syntax and structure
  - Declaring variables and constants in Mojo
  - Control flow and conditional statements
  - Loops and iteration in Mojo

- **Chapter 3: Functions and Modules in Mojo**
  - Defining and using functions in Mojo
  - Exploring built-in functions and libraries
  - Creating and utilizing modules in Mojo
  - Code organization and modular development practices

- **Chapter 4: Object-Oriented Programming in Mojo**
  - Understanding object-oriented principles in Mojo
  - Creating classes and objects in Mojo
  - Encapsulation, inheritance, and polymorphism in Mojo
  - Advanced object-oriented concepts in Mojo

- **Chapter 5: Object-Oriented Programming in Mojo**
  - Fundamental data types in Mojo
  - Manipulating strings, arrays, and dictionaries
  - File I/O operations in Mojo
  - Exploring database connectivity and data handling in Mojo

- **Chapter 6: Web Development with Mojo**
  - Introduction to web development in Mojo
  - Building web applications using Mojo frameworks
  - Working with HTTP requests and responses
  - Integrating databases and APIs in web projects

- **Chapter 7: Mojo and Concurrency**
  - Understanding concurrent programming in Mojo
  - Leveraging parallel processing and multi-threading
  - Synchronization and communication between threads
  - Dealing with common concurrency challenges

- **Chapter 8: Advanced Mojo Techniques**
  - Metaprogramming and code generation in Mojo
  - Creating domain-specific languages (DSLs) with Mojo
  - Debugging and optimizing Mojo code
  - Exploring advanced libraries and frameworks in Mojo

- **Chapter 9: Mojo and the Internet of Things (IoT)**
  - Introduction to IoT and its significance
  - Building IoT applications with Mojo
  - Interacting with sensors, actuators, and IoT devices
  - Integrating cloud services and MQTT in Mojo-based IoT projects

- **Chapter 10: Future of Mojo and Beyond**
  - Current trends and future prospects of Mojo
  - Community and resources for Mojo developers
  - Exploring real-world applications of Mojo
  - What lies ahead: Exciting possibilities with Mojo

- **Conclusion**

CHAPTER 1: INTRODUCING MOJO

WHAT IS MOJO AND WHY IS IT UNIQUE?

Mojo is a dynamic and expressive programming language that stands out for its unique combination of features and design principles. Here's a closer look at what makes Mojo special:

Simplicity and Readability: Mojo places a strong emphasis on clean and readable code. Its syntax is designed to be concise and intuitive, reducing boilerplate and improving code comprehension. This simplicity allows developers to express their ideas in a straightforward and elegant manner.

Expressiveness: Mojo offers a high level of expressiveness, allowing developers to write code that closely matches their thoughts and intentions. It provides powerful constructs such as pattern matching, comprehensions, and first-class functions, enabling developers to solve complex problems with less code.

Multi-paradigm Approach: Mojo blends elements from various programming paradigms, including object-oriented programming (OOP), functional programming, and scripting. This versatility allows developers to choose the best approach for their specific needs and leverage different programming styles within a single language.

Dynamic Typing: Mojo employs dynamic typing, which means that variables do not require explicit type declarations. This flexibility allows for rapid prototyping, easy experimentation, and a more agile development process. It also simplifies certain tasks, such as working with heterogeneous data structures.

Concurrency and Parallelism: Mojo has built-in support for concurrent and parallel programming, making it well-suited for modern computing environments. It provides constructs for managing asynchronous tasks, handling parallel computations, and coordinating concurrent processes, making it easier to develop efficient and scalable software.

Interoperability: Mojo offers seamless integration with existing libraries and frameworks from other languages, allowing developers to leverage the vast ecosystem of tools and resources available. It can interoperate with C/C++, Python, and other popular languages, enabling developers to leverage existing code and extend their capabilities.

Extensibility: Mojo is designed to be extensible, allowing developers to create and share their own libraries and modules. This extensibility fosters a collaborative ecosystem, enabling the community to contribute and build upon each other's work.

In summary, Mojo's simplicity, expressiveness, multi-paradigm approach, dynamic typing, concurrency support, interoperability, and extensibility make it a unique programming language that empowers developers to write elegant, efficient, and flexible code.

A brief history of Mojo and its origins

Mojo has an intriguing history that traces its origins and the factors that influenced its development. Here's a brief overview of the journey of Mojo:

The story of Mojo begins in the early 2010s when a group of passionate programmers recognized the need for a new language that would combine the best aspects of existing languages while addressing some of their limitations. The aim was to create a language that would empower developers with a more expressive and efficient tool for software development.

The core development team, led by visionary programmers, drew inspiration from a range of programming languages, including Python, Ruby, JavaScript, and Haskell. They sought to incorporate the simplicity and readability of Python, the elegance and expressiveness of Ruby, the flexibility of JavaScript, and the functional programming concepts of Haskell.

The project started as an open-source endeavor, with contributions from developers worldwide. The team collaborated closely, engaging in extensive discussions and debates to shape the language's design and syntax. They aimed to strike a balance between simplicity and power, making the language accessible to beginners while satisfying the needs of experienced programmers.

Through iterative development and community feedback, Mojo began to take shape. Early versions focused on defining the language's core features, including its concise syntax, dynamic typing, and support for both functional and object-oriented programming paradigms. As the language matured, new features were added, such as pattern matching, concurrency support, and interoperability with other languages.

The community played a crucial role in the evolution of Mojo. Programmers from different backgrounds shared their experiences, contributed libraries and frameworks, and provided valuable feedback. This collaborative spirit helped refine the language, improve its documentation, and expand its ecosystem.

Mojo gained traction among developers who sought a more expressive and readable alternative to existing languages. Its versatility and power became evident as developers used it to build a wide range of applications, from web development to scientific computing, from automation scripts to game development.

Over time, Mojo's popularity continued to grow, attracting attention from both individual developers and organizations. Its active community and supportive ecosystem fostered further advancements, with new libraries, tools, and frameworks being developed to enhance the language's capabilities.

As of today, Mojo has become an established and respected programming language, known for its simplicity, expressiveness, and flexibility. It continues to evolve, driven by the collaborative efforts of the community and the desire to meet the ever-changing needs of developers.

The history of Mojo exemplifies the spirit of innovation, collaboration, and continuous improvement that underlies its development. From humble beginnings to its present-day status, Mojo remains a testament to the dedication and vision of its creators and the vibrant community that surrounds it.

Understanding the design philosophy behind Mojo

The design philosophy behind Mojo is centered around several key principles that guide its development and shape its unique characteristics. Let's explore the core tenets of Mojo's design philosophy:

Simplicity: Mojo emphasizes simplicity in both syntax and usage. The language aims to have a minimalistic and intuitive syntax that reduces unnecessary complexity and boilerplate code. By keeping things simple, Mojo strives to make programming more accessible and enjoyable for developers of all skill levels.

Readability: Readability is a fundamental aspect of Mojo's design philosophy. Clear, concise, and self-explanatory code is encouraged, enabling developers to easily understand and maintain their programs. By prioritizing readability, Mojo facilitates collaboration, code reviews, and the overall readability of projects.

Expressiveness: Mojo is designed to be expressive, allowing developers to concisely express their ideas and intentions in code. It provides powerful constructs and idioms that help developers solve problems more elegantly and efficiently. This expressiveness promotes code that is not only functional but also highly readable.

Flexibility and Versatility: Mojo embraces a multi-paradigm approach, combining elements of object-oriented programming (OOP), functional programming, and scripting. This flexibility allows developers to choose the most suitable approach for a given problem and encourages the adoption of best practices from different programming paradigms.

Pragmatism: Mojo adopts a pragmatic approach, emphasizing practicality and real-world usage. It aims to provide practical solutions for common programming challenges while avoiding unnecessary complexity. The language encourages developers to focus on solving problems effectively and efficiently.

Interoperability: Mojo values interoperability with other languages and systems. It supports seamless integration with existing libraries and frameworks, allowing developers to leverage external code and resources. This interoperability promotes code reuse, enhances productivity, and facilitates the integration of Mojo into existing software ecosystems.

Community-Driven Development: The Mojo community plays a vital role in shaping the language's direction and development. Feedback and contributions from developers are actively encouraged, fostering a collaborative and inclusive environment. This community-driven approach ensures that Mojo evolves based on the needs and insights of its users.

By adhering to these design principles, Mojo aims to provide developers with a language that is both powerful and enjoyable to work with. Simplicity, readability, expressiveness, flexibility, pragmatism, interoperability, and community involvement are key elements that make Mojo a unique and user-centric programming language.

INSTALLING AND SETTING UP THE MOJO DEVELOPMENT ENVIRONMENT

To get started with Mojo, you'll need to install and set up the Mojo development environment. Here's a step-by-step guide to help you through the process:

Step 1: Install the Mojo Compiler

Visit the official Mojo website or repository to download the Mojo compiler suitable for your operating system (Windows, macOS, or Linux).

Follow the installation instructions specific to your operating system.

Verify the installation by opening a terminal or command prompt and typing mojo --version. You should see the version number of the Mojo compiler if the installation was successful.

Step 2: Install a Text Editor or Integrated Development Environment (IDE)

Choose a text editor or IDE that suits your preferences. Some popular options for editing Mojo code include Visual Studio Code, Sublime Text, Atom, or JetBrains IntelliJ IDEA.

Download and install the chosen text editor or IDE by following the instructions provided on their respective websites.

Step 3: Configure Syntax Highlighting and Autocomplete (optional)

If your chosen text editor or IDE does not have built-in Mojo syntax highlighting and autocomplete, you can install plugins or extensions to enhance the development experience.

Search for the appropriate Mojo language plugin or extension in the plugin marketplace of your text editor or IDE and follow the installation instructions.

Once installed, configure the plugin or extension according to your preferences.

Step 4: Create a Project Directory

Decide on a location where you want to create your Mojo projects.

Open your file explorer or terminal and navigate to the desired location.

Create a new directory for your Mojo project using a command like mkdir my_mojo_project.

Move into the project directory using cd my_mojo_project.

Step 5: Start Coding in Mojo

Open your chosen text editor or IDE.

Use the editor's "Open Folder" or "Open Project" option to open the project directory you created in the previous step.

Create a new file with the .mojo extension, such as main.mojo, and start writing your Mojo code.

Step 6: Compiling and Running Mojo Code

Save your Mojo code file.

Open a terminal or command prompt.

Navigate to the project directory using cd path/to/my_mojo_project.

Compile your Mojo code by running the command mojo build in the terminal.

If there are no compilation errors, you can run your Mojo program by executing the compiled file. For example, if the compiled file is named main.mojo.js, use the command mojo run main.mojo.js to execute it.

Congratulations! You have successfully installed and set up the Mojo development environment. You can now start coding and exploring the capabilities of the Mojo programming language.

CHAPTER 2: GETTING STARTED WITH MOJO

The basics of Mojo syntax and structure

In the dynamic world of programming languages, Mojo stands out with its unique blend of simplicity and power. Whether you're transitioning from another language or starting fresh, understanding Mojo's syntax and structure is pivotal to effective coding. In this guide, we'll delve into the fundamentals.

1. Introduction to Syntax

Mojo's syntax is designed for clarity and conciseness. It embodies the principle of "readability counts," making it easy for developers to write and maintain code.

Whitespace and Indentation: Unlike some languages that rely on braces {} for block delimitation, Mojo uses indentation. This means the amount of whitespace (usually spaces or tabs) before a line of code determines its relationship to the lines around it.

```mojo
if x > 10:
    print("x is large")
```

In the above, the print statement is executed only if x is greater than 10 due to the indentation.

Comments: Any text following a # is considered a comment and is ignored by the compiler.

mojo

```
# This is a comment
print("Hello, Mojo!")  # This prints a greeting
```

2. Declaring Variables

Variables in Mojo don't require a type declaration. The language is dynamically typed, determining the type at runtime based on the value assigned.

mojo

```
name = "Alice"
age = 30
```

Here, name is a string while age is an integer.

3. Data Types

Mojo boasts several fundamental data types:

Numbers: There are integers and floating-point numbers.

mojo

integer_num = 5

float_num = 5.67

Strings: Sequence of characters enclosed in quotes.

mojo

string_variable = "Hello, Mojo!"

Lists: Ordered collection of items, can be mixed type.

mojo

my_list = [1, "Mojo", 3.14]

Dictionaries: Key-value pairs.

mojo

my_dict = {"name": "Alice", "age": 30}

4. Control Flow and Conditional Statements

Control structures guide the flow of execution.

If, Else, Elif: Used for conditional checks.

mojo

if age > 20:

    print("Adult")

```
elif age > 12:
    print("Teenager")
else:
    print("Child")
```

Switch: An alternative to multiple if-elif checks.

mojo

```
switch favorite_fruit:
    case "apple":
        print("You like apples!")
    case "banana":
        print("Bananas are great!")
    default:
        print("All fruits are tasty!")
```

5. Loops and Iteration

Repetition structures, or loops, execute blocks of code multiple times.

For Loop: Iterates over sequences like lists.

mojo

```
for item in my_list:
    print(item)
```

While Loop: Executes as long as a condition remains true.

mojo

```
x = 5
while x > 0:
    print(x)
    x -= 1
```

6. Functions

Functions are reusable blocks of code. In Mojo, you define a function using the def keyword.

mojo

```
def greet(name):
    return "Hello, " + name + "!"
```

To call the function:

mojo

```
message = greet("Alice")
print(message)
```

7. Modules

Modules are separate files containing functions, variables, and classes which can be imported and used in other Mojo programs. For example, if you have a module mathmojo with a function add, you'd use it as:

mojo

import mathmojo

sum = mathmojo.add(5, 3)

Diving into Mojo's syntax and structure unveils a language designed for modern coding needs. Its focus on clarity without compromising on power makes it an appealing choice for developers. As you immerse yourself deeper into Mojo, remember that the foundation lies in its simple yet robust syntax and structure. Happy coding!

DECLARING VARIABLES AND CONSTANTS IN MOJO

In Mojo, you can declare variables and constants using the var and let keywords, respectively. Here's how you can declare variables and constants in Mojo:

Declaring Variables:

var age = 25;   // Variable 'age' with inferred type 'Number'

var name: String = "John";   // Variable 'name' with explicit type annotation 'String'

In the above example, the first line declares a variable named age and assigns it the value 25. Since the type is not explicitly specified, Mojo infers the type as Number. In the second line, the variable name is declared with an explicit type annotation String and assigned the value "John".

Declaring Constants:

let PI = 3.14;   // Constant 'PI' with inferred type 'Number'

let greeting: String = "Hello";   // Constant 'greeting' with explicit type annotation 'String'

The first line declares a constant named PI and assigns it the value 3.14. The type is inferred as Number. The second line declares a constant named greeting with an explicit type annotation String and assigns it the value "Hello".

Type Inference:

Mojo supports type inference, which means the compiler can automatically determine the type of a variable or constant based on the assigned value. If you don't specify the type explicitly, Mojo will infer it from the assigned value.

Example:

var count = 10;   // 'count' is inferred as 'Number'

var message = "Hello"; // 'message' is inferred as 'String'

In the above example, the variable count is inferred as Number because it is assigned the value 10. The variable message is inferred as String because it is assigned the value "Hello".

It's worth noting that in Mojo, you can assign a new value to a variable, but you cannot change the value of a constant once it has been assigned. Variables provide flexibility, whereas constants ensure immutability.

By using variables and constants, you can store and manipulate values in your Mojo programs. Remember to choose meaningful names for your variables and constants to enhance code readability and maintainability.

CONTROL FLOW AND CONDITIONAL STATEMENTS

In Mojo, control flow allows you to make decisions and execute specific blocks of code based on certain conditions. This is achieved through conditional statements. Let's explore the conditional statements and control flow constructs available in Mojo:

If Statements:

The if statement is used to execute a block of code if a given condition is true. It can be followed by an optional else if statement and an optional else statement.

```
var age = 18;

if (age >= 18) {

  print("You are an adult.");

} else {

  print("You are a minor.");

}
```

In the above example, if the age is greater than or equal to 18, the message "You are an adult" will be printed. Otherwise, the message "You are a minor" will be printed.

Switch Statements:

The switch statement allows you to evaluate an expression against multiple cases and execute the corresponding block of code for the matching case.

```
var day = "Tuesday";

switch (day) {

  case "Monday":

    print("It's Monday!");

    break;

  case "Tuesday":

    print("It's Tuesday!");

    break;

  default:
```

```
    print("It's some other day.");
}
```

In the above example, based on the value of the day variable, the corresponding block of code will be executed. In this case, "It's Tuesday!" will be printed.

Loops:

Mojo provides several loop constructs to repeat execution of code until a certain condition is met:

For Loop:

The for loop allows you to iterate over a sequence or execute a block of code a fixed number of times.

```
for (var i = 0; i < 5; i++) {
  print(i);
}
```

n the above example, the loop iterates from i = 0 to i < 5 incrementing i by 1 in each iteration. The value of i will be printed five times.

While Loop:

The while loop executes a block of code as long as a given condition remains true.

```
var counter = 0;
while (counter < 10) {
  print(counter);
```

```
    counter++;
}
```

In the above example, the loop will continue executing as long as the counter variable is less than 10. The value of counter will be printed from 0 to 9.

Do-While Loop:

The do-while loop executes a block of code at least once and then continues to execute as long as a given condition remains true.

```
var x = 0;

do {
  print(x);
  x++;
} while (x < 5);
```

In the above example, the block of code is executed at least once, and then the condition x < 5 is checked. The value of x will be printed from 0 to 4.

These control flow constructs in Mojo allow you to create logic and make decisions based on conditions, repeat code execution, and handle different scenarios within your programs. They provide you with the flexibility to control the flow of execution based on specific conditions or iterations.

CHAPTER 3: FUNCTIONS AND MODULES IN MOJO

Defining and using functions in Mojo

In Mojo, functions are a fundamental building block for organizing and reusing code. They allow you to encapsulate a block of code that performs a specific task or computation. Here's how you can define and use functions in Mojo:

Function Declaration:

Functions are declared using the func keyword, followed by the function name, parameters (optional), return type (optional), and the function body enclosed in curly braces {}.

func greet() {

  print("Hello!");

}

In the above example, we define a function named greet that takes no parameters and has no return type. It simply prints "Hello!" when called.

Function Parameters:

Functions can accept input parameters, which are variables passed to the function for its execution. Parameters are specified inside the parentheses () after the function name.

func greet(name: String) {

  print("Hello, " + name + "!");

}

In this example, the greet function takes a single parameter name of type String. When the function is called, the value passed to name will be used to print a personalized greeting.

Return Values:

Functions can also return values using the return keyword followed by the value to be returned. The return type can be explicitly specified after the parameter list.

func multiply(a: Number, b: Number): Number {

  return a * b;

}

In the above example, the multiply function takes two parameters a and b of type Number and returns their product.

Function Call:

To execute a function, you simply call it by using its name followed by parentheses ().

greet();   // Calls the greet() function

var result = multiply(5, 3);   // Calls the multiply() function and assigns the result to 'result'

In the first line, we call the greet function without any arguments, which will print "Hello!" to the console. In the second line, we call the multiply function with the arguments 5 and 3, and the returned result is assigned to the variable result.

These are the basic steps for defining and using functions in Mojo. Functions help modularize your code, promote reusability, and make your code more organized and readable. They enable you to break down complex tasks into smaller, manageable units of code and promote efficient code reuse.

Exploring built-in functions and libraries

In Mojo, there are built-in functions and libraries available that provide a range of functionality beyond the core language features. These built-in functions and libraries cover various domains such as mathematics, string manipulation, date and time, file handling, and more. Let's explore a few examples:

Mathematical Functions:

Mojo provides built-in mathematical functions such as abs, sqrt, pow, min, max, floor, ceil, and random.

var absolute = abs(-5);   // Returns the absolute value of -5 (5)

var squareRoot = sqrt(25); // Returns the square root of 25 (5)

var power = pow(2, 3);   // Returns 2 raised to the power of 3 (8)

var minimum = min(3, 7);   // Returns the smaller of the two values (3)

var maximum = max(3, 7);   // Returns the larger of the two values (7)

var roundedDown = floor(3.7);   // Returns the rounded-down value (3)

var roundedUp = ceil(3.2);   // Returns the rounded-up value (4)

var randomNum = random();   // Returns a random number between 0 and 1

The above examples demonstrate the usage of some common mathematical functions available in Mojo.

String Functions:

Mojo provides various string manipulation functions, such as length, concat, substring, toUpperCase, toLowerCase, startsWith, endsWith, indexOf, and replace.

var str = "Hello, World!";

var length = length(str);   // Returns the length of the string (13)

var concatenated = concat("Hello", " ", "World"); // Returns the concatenated string ("Hello World")

var substring = substring(str, 0, 5);   // Returns the substring from index 0 to 4 ("Hello")

var upperCase = toUpperCase(str);   // Converts the string to uppercase ("HELLO, WORLD!")

var lowerCase = toLowerCase(str);   // Converts the string to lowercase ("hello, world!")

var startsWithHello = startsWith(str, "Hello");   // Checks if the string starts with "Hello" (true)

var endsWithWorld = endsWith(str, "World");   // Checks if the string ends with "World" (false)

var indexOfComma = indexOf(str, ",");   // Returns the index of the first occurrence of "," (5)

var replaced = replace(str, "World", "Universe");   // Replaces "World" with "Universe" ("Hello, Universe!")

These functions allow you to manipulate and extract information from strings efficiently.

Date and Time Functions:

Mojo provides functions to work with date and time, including now, format, parse, and various methods to extract specific components of a date.

var currentTimestamp = now();   // Returns the current timestamp

var formattedDate = format(currentTimestamp, "yyyy-MM-dd");   // Formats the date as "YYYY-MM-DD"

var parsedDate = parse("2022-01-01", "yyyy-MM-dd");   // Parses the date string into a timestamp

var year = getYear(currentTimestamp);   // Extracts the year from a timestamp

var month = getMonth(currentTimestamp);   // Extracts the month from a timestamp

var day = getDay(currentTimestamp);   // Extracts the day from a timestamp

These functions allow you to perform date and time-related operations and manipulate date formats.

File Handling Functions:

Mojo provides functions for file handling operations, including reading from and writing to files. These functions are part of the standard library and can be accessed through the File class.

var file = File("data.txt");   // Creates a File object with the specified file path

var content = file.read();   // Reads the content of the file

file.write("Hello, Mojo!");   // Writes content to the file

These functions allow you to interact with files, read their contents, and write data to them.

These are just a few examples of the built-in functions and libraries available in Mojo. The standard library provides a rich set of functionality that you can leverage to simplify and enhance your code. Additionally, Mojo allows you to create and import your own custom libraries to encapsulate and reuse code specific to your project's requirements.

Creating and utilizing modules in Mojo

In Mojo, modules are used to organize and encapsulate related code into separate files, promoting modularity and code reusability. Modules allow you to define classes, functions, and variables that can be imported and used in other parts of your program. Here's how you can create and utilize modules in Mojo:

Creating a Module:

To create a module, you need to create a separate file with a .mojo extension. In this file, you can define your classes, functions, and variables.

example_module.mojo:

```
class Person {
  var name: String;
  var age: Number;

  func introduce() {
    print("My name is " + name + " and I am " + age + " years old.");
  }
}
```

```
func addNumbers(a: Number, b: Number): Number {
  return a + b;
}


let PI = 3.14;
```

In the above example, we define a Person class, a addNumbers function, and a constant PI in the example_module.mojo file.

Importing a Module:

To use the code defined in a module, you need to import it into your main program file using the import statement.

main_program.mojo:

```
import "example_module.mojo";


var john = new Person();
john.name = "John";
john.age = 25;
john.introduce();


var result = addNumbers(5, 3);
print(result);
```

```
print(PI);
```

In the main_program.mojo file, we import the example_module.mojo module using the import statement. We can then create an instance of the Person class, call its methods, use the addNumbers function, and access the PI constant defined in the module.

Running the Program:

To run the program, you need to execute the main program file, which in this case is main_program.mojo. Depending on your development environment or command-line setup, you can run the program by executing the appropriate command.

```
mojo run main_program.mojo
```

The above command executes the main_program.mojo file, which includes the imported module example_module.mojo. You will see the output of the program based on the code defined in the files.

By creating and utilizing modules, you can organize your code into logical units, promote code reuse, and enhance the maintainability of your Mojo programs. Modules provide a way to separate concerns and make your codebase more modular and scalable.

Code organization and modular development practices

Code organization and modular development practices are essential for creating maintainable and scalable projects in Mojo. Here are some practices and techniques to help you organize your code effectively:

Modularization:

Break your code into modules or files based on functionality and purpose. Each module should have a specific responsibility or provide a cohesive set of features. This allows for better code separation and makes it easier to navigate and maintain the project.

Naming Conventions:

Use consistent and meaningful names for your modules, classes, functions, and variables. Clear and descriptive naming makes your code more readable and helps others understand its purpose.

Directory Structure:

Establish a logical directory structure for your project. Group related modules and files into directories based on their purpose or feature set. For larger projects, consider using subdirectories to further organize the codebase.

Encapsulation:

Encapsulate related functionality into classes and modules. Use classes to define objects with properties and methods that represent real-world entities or concepts. Encapsulation helps in achieving modular and reusable code.

Separation of Concerns:

Follow the principle of separation of concerns, where each module or class should have a single responsibility. Avoid mixing unrelated functionality in a single module, as it can lead to code complexity and maintainability issues.

Dependency Management:

Identify and manage dependencies between modules. Clearly define dependencies and ensure that modules rely on abstractions rather than concrete implementations. This allows for flexible and interchangeable components.

Documentation:

Document your code to provide insights into its functionality, purpose, and usage. Include comments, docstrings, and README files to explain the intention and usage of modules, classes, and functions. Well-documented code improves readability and facilitates collaboration.

Testing:

Implement unit tests to verify the correctness of your code. Create test modules or files that exercise the functionality of your modules and classes. Testing helps ensure that your code behaves as expected and provides a safety net for refactoring and future modifications.

Version Control:

Utilize a version control system (e.g., Git) to track changes to your codebase. Maintain a clean commit history and use branching and merging strategies to facilitate collaboration and manage code changes effectively.

Reusability:

Identify common functionalities or patterns in your code and extract them into reusable modules or libraries. Encapsulate generic functionality into separate modules that can be easily imported and reused in multiple projects.

By following these practices, you can create a well-organized and maintainable codebase in Mojo. Consistent code organization and modular development practices contribute to better code readability, maintainability, and scalability, enabling you to work efficiently and collaborate effectively on your projects.

CHAPTER 4: OBJECT-ORIENTED PROGRAMMING IN MOJO

Understanding object-oriented principles in Mojo

In Mojo, object-oriented programming (OOP) principles provide a way to structure and organize code by encapsulating data and behavior into objects. OOP promotes modularity, reusability, and maintainability of code. Here are the key object-oriented principles in Mojo:

Classes and Objects:

Classes are the blueprints or templates that define the properties and behavior of objects. Objects are instances of classes that represent specific entities or concepts. Classes and objects are fundamental to OOP in Mojo.

```
class Person {
  var name: String;
  var age: Number;

  func introduce() {
    print("My name is " + name + " and I am " + age + " years old.");
  }
```

}

var john = new Person();

john.name = "John";

john.age = 25;

john.introduce();

In the example above, the Person class defines properties name and age, as well as a method introduce(). An object john is created based on the Person class, and its properties are set and method is called.

Encapsulation:

Encapsulation is the principle of bundling related data and methods together into a single unit (a class) and hiding the internal details from the outside world. This protects the integrity of the data and provides controlled access through methods.

Inheritance:

Inheritance allows a class to inherit properties and methods from another class, enabling code reuse and the creation of specialized classes. The derived class (subclass) inherits the characteristics of the base class (superclass) and can extend or override its behavior.

class Employee : Person {

  var employeeId: String;

  func displayEmployeeInfo() {

```
    print("Employee ID: " + employeeId);
  }
}
```

```
var alice = new Employee();
alice.name = "Alice";
alice.age = 30;
alice.employeeId = "12345";
alice.introduce();
alice.displayEmployeeInfo();
```

In the example above, the Employee class inherits from the Person class. It adds a new property employeeId and a new method displayEmployeeInfo(). The object alice is an instance of the Employee class and can access both the inherited and derived properties and methods.

Polymorphism:

Polymorphism allows objects of different classes to be treated as instances of a common superclass. This enables writing code that can work with objects of multiple types, providing flexibility and extensibility.

```
func printInfo(person: Person) {
  person.introduce();
}
```

```
var bob = new Person();

bob.name = "Bob";

bob.age = 35;


var mary = new Employee();

mary.name = "Mary";

mary.age = 40;

mary.employeeId = "98765";


printInfo(bob);

printInfo(mary);
```

In the example above, the printInfo() function accepts a Person object as an argument. Both bob (of type Person) and mary (of type Employee) can be passed to the function, demonstrating polymorphism. The function can work with objects of different types as long as they are derived from the Person class.

Abstraction:

Abstraction focuses on providing a simplified interface to interact with complex systems. It involves hiding unnecessary implementation details and exposing only the essential features and functionality.

```
abstract class Shape {
  abstract func calculateArea(): Number;
}
```

```
class Rectangle : Shape {

  var width: Number;

  var height: Number;


  func calculateArea(): Number {

    return width * height;

  }

}


var rectangle = new Rectangle();

rectangle.width = 5;

rectangle.height = 10;

var area = rectangle.calculateArea();
```

In the example above, the Shape class is abstract and defines an abstract method calculateArea(). The Rectangle class inherits from Shape and provides an implementation of the calculateArea() method. By using abstraction, the client code interacts with the abstract Shape class without needing to know the specific implementation details of the Rectangle class.

These object-oriented principles in Mojo provide a solid foundation for organizing and structuring code, promoting reusability, maintainability, and extensibility. By leveraging classes, inheritance, polymorphism, encapsulation, and abstraction, you can create well-designed and modular applications.

CREATING CLASSES AND OBJECTS IN MOJO

In Mojo, you can create classes to define the properties and behavior of objects. Objects are instances of classes that represent specific entities or concepts. Here's how you can create classes and objects in Mojo:

Class Definition:

To define a class, use the class keyword followed by the class name and a block of code that represents the class's properties and methods.

```
class Person {
  var name: String;
  var age: Number;

  func introduce() {
    print("My name is " + name + " and I am " + age + " years old.");
  }
}
```

In the example above, we define a Person class with two properties (name and age) and a method (introduce()). The name property is of type String, and the age property is of type Number.

Creating Objects:

To create an object, use the new keyword followed by the class name and parentheses. Assign the created object to a variable for later use.

var john = new Person();

In the example above, we create a new object john based on the Person class.

Accessing Properties and Methods:

Once an object is created, you can access its properties and methods using the dot notation (.).

john.name = "John";

john.age = 25;

john.introduce();

In the example above, we assign values to the name and age properties of the john object. We then call the introduce() method on the john object, which prints a message to the console.

You can create multiple objects from the same class, each with its own set of property values. Each object will have its own separate memory space to store its property values.

```
var alice = new Person();

alice.name = "Alice";

alice.age = 30;

alice.introduce();
```

In the example above, we create another object alice based on the Person class and set its name and age properties. We then call the introduce() method on the alice object.

By creating classes and objects, you can define the structure and behavior of your entities and create instances of those entities as needed. Classes and objects provide a powerful way to organize and manipulate data in your Mojo programs.

Encapsulation, inheritance, and polymorphism in Mojo

Encapsulation, inheritance, and polymorphism are fundamental concepts in object-oriented programming (OOP). Let's explore how these concepts can be implemented in Mojo:

Encapsulation:

Encapsulation involves bundling data and methods together within a class, hiding the internal details of an object, and providing controlled access to its properties and methods. In Mojo, you can achieve encapsulation by defining private and public access modifiers.

```
class Person {
  private var name: String;
  private var age: Number;

  func setName(newName: String) {
    name = newName;
  }

  func setAge(newAge: Number) {
    age = newAge;
  }

  func introduce() {
    print("My name is " + name + " and I am " + age + " years old.");
  }
}
```

In the example above, the name and age properties are marked as private, which means they can only be accessed within the class itself. The setName() and setAge() methods provide a controlled way to modify these properties from outside the class.

Inheritance:

Inheritance allows you to create a new class (subclass) based on an existing class (superclass). The subclass inherits the properties and methods of the superclass, and it can add its own properties and methods or override the inherited ones.

```
class Employee : Person {

  private var employeeId: String;


  func setEmployeeId(id: String) {

    employeeId = id;

  }


  override func introduce() {

    super.introduce();

    print("Employee ID: " + employeeId);

  }

}
```

In the example above, the Employee class inherits from the Person class using the : symbol. The Employee class adds a new private property employeeId and a new method setEmployeeId(). The introduce() method is overridden to include additional information specific to employees. The super.introduce() call invokes the introduce() method of the superclass.

Polymorphism:

Polymorphism allows objects of different classes to be treated as instances of a common superclass. In Mojo, polymorphism is achieved by defining a common interface or using inheritance.

func printInfo(person: Person) {

  person.introduce();

}

var john = new Person();

john.setName("John");

john.setAge(25);

var alice = new Employee();

alice.setName("Alice");

alice.setAge(30);

alice.setEmployeeId("12345");

printInfo(john);

printInfo(alice);

In the example above, the printInfo() function accepts a Person object as a parameter. Both the Person and Employee objects can be passed to this function because Employee is a subclass of Person. The introduce() method is called on each object, and the appropriate implementation is executed based on the actual type of the object.

By utilizing encapsulation, inheritance, and polymorphism, you can create modular, extensible, and reusable code in Mojo. These concepts enable you to design object-oriented programs that are easier to maintain, enhance, and understand.

ADVANCED OBJECT-ORIENTED CONCEPTS IN MOJO

In addition to encapsulation, inheritance, and polymorphism, Mojo supports several other advanced object-oriented concepts. Let's explore some of these concepts:

Abstract Classes:

Abstract classes are classes that cannot be instantiated directly, but serve as a blueprint for derived classes. They can contain both abstract and non-abstract methods. Abstract methods are declared without an implementation and must be overridden in derived classes. Abstract classes are defined using the abstract keyword.

abstract class Shape {

```
  abstract func calculateArea(): Number;

  func display() {
    print("This is a shape.");
  }
}
```

In the example above, the Shape class is defined as abstract, and it declares an abstract method calculateArea() and a non-abstract method display(). Any class that extends the Shape class must provide an implementation for the calculateArea() method.

Interfaces:

Interfaces define a contract that classes can implement. They consist of abstract method declarations without any implementation. Classes that implement an interface must provide the implementation for all the methods defined in the interface. Interfaces are defined using the interface keyword.

```
interface Drawable {
  func draw(): String;
}
```

In the example above, the Drawable interface declares a single method draw(). Classes that implement the Drawable interface must provide an implementation for this method.

Mixins:

Mixins are reusable code modules that can be mixed into classes to provide additional functionality. They allow for code reuse across multiple classes without requiring inheritance. Mixins are defined using the mixin keyword.

```
mixin Loggable {
  func log(message: String) {
    print("Log: " + message);
  }
}
```

In the example above, the Loggable mixin provides a log() method. It can be mixed into multiple classes, allowing them to log messages without inheritance.

Method Overloading:

Method overloading allows a class to define multiple methods with the same name but different parameter lists. The methods can have different numbers of parameters or different parameter types. The appropriate method is called based on the arguments provided.

```
class Calculator {
  func add(a: Number, b: Number) {
    return a + b;
  }

  func add(a: String, b: String) {
```

        return a + b;

  }

}

In the example above, the Calculator class defines two add() methods, one for adding numbers and another for concatenating strings. The appropriate method is called based on the argument types at the call site.

These advanced object-oriented concepts in Mojo provide additional flexibility and power in designing and structuring your code. By utilizing abstract classes, interfaces, mixins, and method overloading, you can create more modular and reusable code and design more flexible and extensible systems.

CHAPTER 5: OBJECT-ORIENTED PROGRAMMING IN MOJO

FUNDAMENTAL DATA TYPES IN MOJO

In Mojo, there are several fundamental data types that you can use to store and manipulate different kinds of data. Here are the fundamental data types available in Mojo:

Number:

The Number type represents numeric values, including integers and floating-point numbers.

var count: Number = 10;

var pi: Number = 3.14159;

String:

The String type represents a sequence of characters enclosed in double quotes (").

var message: String = "Hello, Mojo!";

Boolean:

The Boolean type represents a logical value, either true or false.

var isTrue: Boolean = true;

var isFalse: Boolean = false;

Array:

The Array type represents an ordered collection of values. Arrays can hold elements of any type.

var numbers: Array<Number> = [1, 2, 3, 4, 5];

var names: Array<String> = ["Alice", "Bob", "Charlie"];

Map:

The Map type represents an associative array or dictionary that stores key-value pairs. Keys must be unique within the map.

var ages: Map<String, Number> = {"Alice": 25, "Bob": 30, "Charlie": 35};

Null:

The Null type represents the absence of a value.

var data: Null = null;

Undefined:

The Undefined type represents an uninitialized variable or an absent property value.

var x: Undefined;

These fundamental data types in Mojo provide the building blocks for storing, manipulating, and representing different kinds of data in your programs. You can use these data types to declare variables, function parameters, and return types to work with various data in your Mojo code.

MANIPULATING STRINGS, ARRAYS, AND DICTIONARIES

In Mojo, you can manipulate strings, arrays, and dictionaries using various built-in methods and operators. Here are some common operations you can perform on these data types:

Manipulating Strings:

Concatenation: You can concatenate strings using the + operator or the concat() method.

var firstName: String = "John";

var lastName: String = "Doe";

var fullName: String = firstName + " " + lastName;

// Result: "John Doe"

var greeting: String = firstName.concat(" ", lastName);

// Result: "John Doe"

Length: You can get the length of a string using the length property.

var message: String = "Hello, Mojo!";

var length: Number = message.length;

// Result: 13

Substring: You can extract a substring from a string using the substring() method.

var message: String = "Hello, Mojo!";

var substring: String = message.substring(7, 12);

// Result: "Mojo"

Searching: You can search for substrings within a string using methods like indexOf() or includes().

var message: String = "Hello, Mojo!";

var index: Number = message.indexOf("Mojo");

// Result: 7

var includesMojo: Boolean = message.includes("Mojo");

// Result: true

Manipulating Arrays:

Accessing Elements: You can access individual elements in an array using index notation ([]).

var numbers: Array<Number> = [1, 2, 3, 4, 5];

var firstNumber: Number = numbers[0];

// Result: 1

Modifying Elements: You can modify elements in an array by assigning new values to specific indices.

var numbers: Array<Number> = [1, 2, 3, 4, 5];

numbers[2] = 10;

// numbers is now [1, 2, 10, 4, 5]

Adding and Removing Elements: You can add elements to the end of an array using the push() method and remove elements from the end using the pop() method.

var numbers: Array<Number> = [1, 2, 3];

numbers.push(4);

// numbers is now [1, 2, 3, 4]

var removedNumber: Number = numbers.pop();

// removedNumber is 4, and numbers is now [1, 2, 3]

Manipulating Dictionaries:

Accessing Values: You can access the value associated with a specific key in a dictionary using index notation ([]).

var ages: Map<String, Number> = {"Alice": 25, "Bob": 30, "Charlie": 35};

var aliceAge: Number = ages["Alice"];

// Result: 25

Modifying Values: You can modify the value associated with a key in a dictionary by assigning a new value.

var ages: Map<String, Number> = {"Alice": 25, "Bob": 30};

ages["Alice"] = 26;

// ages is now {"Alice": 26, "Bob": 30}

Adding and Removing Entries: You can add new key-value pairs to a dictionary by assigning a value to a new key. To remove an entry, use the delete keyword.

var ages: Map<String, Number> = {"Alice": 25, "Bob": 30};

ages["Charlie"] = 35;

// ages is now {"Alice": 25, "Bob": 30, "Charlie": 35}

delete ages["Bob"];

// ages is now {"Alice": 25, "Charlie": 35}

These are just a few examples of the operations you can perform on strings, arrays, and dictionaries in Mojo. There are many more methods and techniques available, so feel free to explore the Mojo documentation for a comprehensive list of functions and operators for each data type.

FILE I/O OPERATIONS IN MOJO

In Mojo, you can perform file input/output (I/O) operations to read from and write to files on the system. Here's an overview of file I/O operations in Mojo:

Reading from a File:

To read from a file, you can use the File.read() method, which reads the contents of a file and returns them as a string.

var file = new File("path/to/file.txt");

var content = file.read();

print(content);

The above code creates a new File object by providing the path to the file. The read() method is called on the file object to read its contents, which are then stored in the content variable.

Writing to a File:

To write data to a file, you can use the File.write() method, which takes a string as input and writes it to the file.

var file = new File("path/to/file.txt");

var data = "This is some data to write to the file.";

file.write(data);

In the above example, the File object is created for the target file. The write() method is called on the file object, passing the data to be written as a string.

Appending to a File:

If you want to append data to an existing file, you can use the File.append() method, which works similar to the write() method but appends the data to the end of the file instead of overwriting it.

var file = new File("path/to/file.txt");

var data = "This is some additional data.";

file.append(data);

The append() method appends the data to the existing content of the file.

Checking File Existence:

You can check if a file exists before performing any I/O operations on it using the File.exists() method.

var file = new File("path/to/file.txt");

var exists = file.exists();

if (exists) {

  // File exists, perform operations

} else {

  // File does not exist

}

The exists() method returns a boolean value indicating whether the file exists or not.

Error Handling:

It's important to handle errors that can occur during file I/O operations. You can use try-catch blocks to catch and handle exceptions thrown during file operations.

```
try {
  var file = new File("path/to/file.txt");
  var content = file.read();
  print(content);
} catch (error) {
  print("An error occurred: " + error.message);
}
```

In the above code, the file reading operation is wrapped within a try block, and any exceptions are caught in the catch block. The error message is then printed for debugging or error-handling purposes.

Remember to handle file I/O operations with care, considering factors such as file permissions and proper error handling to ensure reliable and secure file manipulation in your Mojo programs.

EXPLORING DATABASE CONNECTIVITY AND DATA HANDLING IN MOJO

In Mojo, you can connect to databases and handle data using database connectivity libraries. One popular library for database connectivity in Mojo is mojo-db. It provides a convenient interface for connecting to various databases and performing database operations. Here's an overview of how you can work with databases in Mojo using mojo-db:

Installing mojo-db:

Before you can use mojo-db, you need to install it as a dependency in your Mojo project. You can do this using the package manager mpm:

mpm install mojo-db

This command installs the mojo-db library and its dependencies in your project.

Connecting to a Database:

Once mojo-db is installed, you can connect to a database using the appropriate driver and connection settings. Here's an example of connecting to a MySQL database:

import mojo.db;

var connection = new DatabaseConnection({

  driver: "mysql",

  host: "localhost",

  port: 3306,

```
  username: "your_username",
  password: "your_password",
  database: "your_database"
});
```

connection.connect();

In the above code, the DatabaseConnection object is created with the necessary connection settings for the MySQL database. The connect() method is called to establish the connection.

Executing Queries:

After establishing the database connection, you can execute queries to retrieve or modify data. Here's an example of executing a SELECT query:

var query = "SELECT * FROM users";

var result = connection.query(query);

```
while (result.hasNext()) {
  var row = result.next();
  // Process each row of data
}
```

result.close();

In the above code, the query() method is called on the database connection to execute the SELECT query. The result object provides access to the retrieved data. You can iterate over the rows using the hasNext() and next() methods, and perform operations on each row. Finally, remember to close the result set using the close() method.

Executing Prepared Statements:

To handle dynamic queries or queries with parameters, you can use prepared statements. Here's an example:

var query = "INSERT INTO users (name, email) VALUES (?, ?)";

var statement = connection.prepare(query);

var name = "John Doe";

var email = "johndoe@example.com";

statement.bindParams([name, email]);

statement.execute();

statement.close();

In the above code, a prepared statement is created using the prepare() method, and placeholders (?) are used for the values. The bindParams() method is used to bind the actual values to the placeholders. Finally, the statement is executed using the execute() method.

Handling Errors:

When working with databases, it's important to handle errors that may occur during database operations. You can use try-catch blocks to catch and handle exceptions thrown by mojo-db methods.

```
try {

  // Database operations

} catch (error) {

  print("An error occurred: " + error.message);

}
```

In the above code, the database operations are wrapped within a try block, and any exceptions are caught in the catch block. The error message can be printed or handled as per your application's requirements.

lease note that the specific usage and syntax may vary depending on the database driver you're using with mojo-db. It's recommended to refer to the mojo-db documentation and the documentation of the specific database driver for detailed information and examples.

By utilizing database connectivity libraries like mojo-db, you can interact with databases, execute queries, handle data, and perform various database operations in your Mojo applications.

CHAPTER 6: WEB DEVELOPMENT WITH MOJO

INTRODUCTION TO WEB DEVELOPMENT IN MOJO

Web development in Mojo involves building web applications and websites using the Mojo web framework. Mojo provides a powerful and flexible set of tools and features for creating server-side applications, handling HTTP requests and responses, and generating dynamic web content. Here's an introduction to web development in Mojo:

Setting up a Mojo Web Project:

To get started with web development in Mojo, you'll need to set up a new Mojo web project. You can create a new project using the Mojo command-line interface (CLI) tool.

```
mojo generate app MyWebApp
```

This command creates a new Mojo web application named "MyWebApp" in a directory with the same name.

Handling Routes and Requests:

In Mojo, routes define the URLs that your application will respond to and the actions to be taken for each route. Routes are defined in the startup method of your application class.

```
class MyApp extends Mojo::Base {

  method startup {

    my $r = $self->routes;

    $r->get('/')->to('example#welcome');

  }

}
```

In the above code, a route is defined for the root URL ("/"), and it is associated with the welcome action in the example controller.

Creating Controllers and Actions:

Controllers handle the logic and actions for specific routes. Each action within a controller corresponds to a specific functionality or behavior of your web application.

```
package MyApp::Controller::Example;


use Mojo::Base 'Mojolicious::Controller';


sub welcome {

  my $self = shift;
```

```perl
  $self->render(text => 'Welcome to Mojo!');
}
```

1;

In the above code, a controller named Example is created, and it inherits from Mojolicious::Controller. The welcome action is defined, which simply renders a text response of "Welcome to Mojo!".

Rendering Views:

Views in Mojo are used to generate the HTML content that will be sent back to the client. You can use various templating systems supported by Mojo, such as Template Toolkit, to render dynamic content.

```perl
sub welcome {
  my $self = shift;
  $self->render(template => 'example/welcome');
}
```

In the above code, the render method is called with the template parameter set to 'example/welcome'. This will render the corresponding template file named welcome.html.ep within the example folder.

Serving Static Files:

Mojo allows you to serve static files such as CSS, JavaScript, and images directly from your web application. You can define a static route in the startup method to specify the location of your static files.

```
$r->get('/public/*file')->to('example#serve_static');
```

In the above code, a static route is defined to match any request starting with '/public/' and associate it with the serve_static action in the example controller.

Starting the Web Server:

Finally, you can start the Mojo web server to run your application.

```
mojo server
```

This command starts the development server, and your web application will be accessible at the specified URL (usually http://localhost:3000).

This is just a brief introduction to web development in Mojo. There is much more you can do with Mojo, including handling form submissions, authentication, working with databases, and more. The Mojo documentation provides detailed information and examples on all aspects of web development using Mojo.

Building web applications using Mojo frameworks

Building web applications using the Mojo web framework involves utilizing the features and components provided by Mojo to handle HTTP requests, implement routes, render views, manage sessions, and interact with databases. Here's an overview of the steps involved in building a web application using Mojo:

Define Routes:

Routes determine how your application responds to different URLs. In Mojo, you define routes in the startup method of your application class.

```
sub startup {
  my $self = shift;
  my $r = $self->routes;

  # Define routes here
  $r->get('/')->to('example#welcome');
}
```

In the above code, a route is defined for the root URL ("/") and associated with the welcome action in the example controller.

Create Controllers:

Controllers handle the logic and actions for specific routes. Each action within a controller corresponds to a specific functionality or behavior of your web application.

```perl
package MyApp::Controller::Example;

use Mojo::Base 'Mojolicious::Controller';

sub welcome {
  my $self = shift;
  $self->render(template => 'example/welcome');
}

1;
```

In the above code, a controller named Example is created, and it inherits from Mojolicious::Controller. The welcome action renders a template named 'example/welcome'.

Render Views:

Views in Mojo are used to generate the HTML content that will be sent back to the client. You can use Mojo's built-in template system, such as Embedded Perl (EP), to render dynamic content.

```perl
sub welcome {
  my $self = shift;
  $self->render(template => 'example/welcome');
}
```

In the above code, the render method is called with the template parameter set to 'example/welcome'. This will render the corresponding template file named welcome.html.ep within the example folder.

Handle Form Submissions:

Mojo provides convenient methods for handling form submissions. You can access form data and perform validation within your controller actions.

```perl
sub process_form {
    my $self = shift;
    my $username = $self->param('username');
    # Process form data and perform validation
}
```

In the above code, the param method is used to access the value of the 'username' field submitted in a form.

Interact with Databases:

Mojo has support for connecting to databases and performing database operations. You can use Mojo's database connectivity libraries, such as mojo-db, to interact with databases and execute queries.

```perl
sub get_users {
    my $self = shift;
    my $users = $self->app->db->select('users');
```

```
    # Process user data retrieved from the database
}
```

In the above code, the select method is called on the database object to retrieve user data from the 'users' table.

Implement Authentication and Sessions:

Mojo provides components for implementing user authentication and managing sessions. You can utilize these components to handle user logins, store session data, and enforce access controls.

```
sub login {
    my $self = shift;
    my $username = $self->param('username');
    my $password = $self->param('password');
    # Verify user credentials and log them in
}
```

In the above code, the param method is used to retrieve the values of the 'username' and 'password' fields from a login form.

Start the Web Server:

Once you have defined routes, controllers, and actions, you can start the Mojo web server to run your application.

```
./myapp.pl daemon
```

This command starts the development server, and your web application will be accessible at the specified URL (usually http://localhost:3000).

These are just some of the fundamental steps involved in building web applications using the Mojo framework. Mojo provides many more features and components that you can explore and utilize as per your application's requirements. The Mojo documentation is a valuable resource that provides detailed information, examples, and best practices for building web applications with Mojo.

Working with HTTP requests and responses

In Mojo, working with HTTP requests and responses is a fundamental aspect of building web applications. Mojo provides a set of convenient methods and components for handling and manipulating HTTP requests and responses. Here's an overview of how you can work with HTTP requests and responses in Mojo:

Accessing Request Information:

Inside a controller action, you can access various details about the incoming HTTP request, such as the request method, URL parameters, query parameters, form data, headers, and more.

sub process_request {

  my $self = shift;

```perl
  # Access request information
  my $method = $self->req->method;
  my $url_param = $self->param('id');
  my $query_param = $self->req->query_params->param('search');
  my $header_value = $self->req->headers->header('User-Agent');

  # Process the request
  # ...
}
```

In the above code, $self->req gives you access to the request object, and you can use its methods to retrieve information about the request.

Manipulating Request Parameters:

You can access and manipulate request parameters, including URL parameters, query parameters, and form data.

```perl
sub process_request {
  my $self = shift;

  # Access request parameters
  my $url_param = $self->param('id');
  my $query_param = $self->param('search');
  my $form_data = $self->req->body_params->param('name');
```

```perl
  # Manipulate request parameters

  $self->param('id', 123);  # Set a URL parameter value

  $self->param(search => 'keyword');  # Set a query parameter value


  # Process the request

  # ...
}
```

In the above code, $self->param allows you to access and modify request parameters.

Building Responses:

You can construct HTTP responses to send back to the client. This includes setting response headers, status codes, and the response body.

```perl
sub generate_response {
  my $self = shift;


  # Set response headers

  $self->res->headers->header('Content-Type' => 'text/html');


  # Set response status code

  $self->res->code(200);
```

```perl
  # Set response body
  $self->render(text => 'Hello, Mojo!');

  # You can also use a template to render the response
  $self->render(template => 'greeting', name => 'Mojo');

  # Or render a JSON response
  $self->render(json => { message => 'Hello, Mojo!' });
}
```

In the above code, you can set response headers and status code using $self->res->headers and $self->res->code, respectively. The render method allows you to generate the response body, whether it's plain text, HTML, a template, or JSON.

Redirection:

Mojo provides methods for redirecting the client to a different URL.

```perl
sub perform_redirection {
  my $self = shift;

  # Redirect the client to a different URL
  $self->redirect_to('/new-url');
}
```

In the above code, the redirect_to method is used to redirect the client to the specified URL.

Accessing Cookies:

You can read and write cookies associated with the request and response.

```perl
sub handle_cookies {
  my $self = shift;

  # Read a cookie value
  my $cookie_value = $self->cookie('my_cookie');

  # Set a cookie
  $self->cookie(my_cookie => 'cookie_value');
}
```

In the above code, $self->cookie allows you to read and write cookies.

These are some basic examples of working with HTTP requests and responses in Mojo. Mojo provides a rich set of methods and components for handling various aspects of HTTP communication. You can refer to the Mojo documentation for more details and advanced usage of handling requests and responses.

CHAPTER 7: MOJO AND CONCURRENCY

Understanding concurrent programming in Mojo

Concurrent programming in Mojo involves executing multiple tasks simultaneously to improve performance and responsiveness. Mojo provides various tools and features to facilitate concurrent programming. Here are some key aspects of concurrent programming in Mojo:

Non-blocking I/O:

Mojo utilizes non-blocking I/O operations, which allows it to handle multiple I/O tasks concurrently without blocking the execution flow. Non-blocking I/O operations ensure that your application can efficiently handle multiple simultaneous requests without waiting for each operation to complete before moving on to the next.

Asynchronous Programming:

Asynchronous programming is a technique used in Mojo to perform tasks concurrently without blocking the execution flow. Mojo utilizes asynchronous constructs such as Promises, Futures, and asynchronous functions to handle concurrent operations. Asynchronous programming enables you to execute multiple tasks concurrently and handle the results once they become available.

Event Loop:

Mojo operates on an event loop, which is responsible for managing and dispatching events in a non-blocking manner. The event loop is at the core of Mojo's concurrent programming model and allows you to handle multiple events and I/O operations concurrently.

Parallel Execution:

Mojo provides utilities for executing tasks in parallel. You can use functions like Mojo::IOLoop->delay and Mojo::Promise->all to execute multiple tasks concurrently and wait for all of them to complete. This allows you to improve the overall performance and efficiency of your application.

Coroutines:

Mojo supports the use of coroutines, which are special functions that can be suspended and resumed. Coroutines allow you to write code that appears sequential but executes concurrently. You can use the Mojo::IOLoop->start and Mojo::IOLoop->stop methods to control the execution of coroutines and coordinate concurrent tasks.

WebSockets:

Mojo provides built-in support for WebSockets, which enables real-time, bidirectional communication between the client and the server. WebSockets allow for concurrent communication between the client and the server without the need for multiple HTTP requests.

By leveraging these features and techniques, you can write highly concurrent and efficient applications in Mojo. It's important to note that concurrent programming requires careful consideration of synchronization, resource sharing, and error handling to ensure the correctness and stability of your code. The Mojo documentation provides detailed information and examples on how to effectively utilize concurrent programming techniques in Mojo.

LEVERAGING PARALLEL PROCESSING AND MULTI-THREADING

In Mojo, leveraging parallel processing and multi-threading can significantly improve the performance and efficiency of your applications. While Mojo itself is primarily based on an event-driven model, you can still utilize parallel processing and multi-threading techniques for certain computationally intensive or blocking tasks. Here are a few approaches you can take:

Forking Processes:

Mojo allows you to fork child processes to perform parallel processing. You can use Perl's fork function to create child processes, where each child process can handle a specific task independently. This technique is useful for tasks that can be easily divided into independent subtasks.

```perl
use Mojo::Base -strict;

# Create child processes to perform parallel processing

for (1..$num_processes) {
```

```perl
  my $pid = fork();
  if ($pid) {
    # Parent process
  }
  elsif ($pid == 0) {
    # Child process - perform the task
    # ...
    exit;
  }
  else {
    # Fork failed
    die "Failed to fork: $!";
  }
}
```

In the above code, multiple child processes are forked, and each child process executes a specific task independently.

Mojo::IOLoop->subprocess:

Mojo provides the Mojo::IOLoop->subprocess method, which allows you to execute external commands or scripts asynchronously in separate processes. This approach is useful when you need to run external commands in parallel and asynchronously.

```perl
use Mojo::IOLoop;

# Execute commands asynchronously in separate processes
Mojo::IOLoop->subprocess(
  sub {
    my ($subprocess, $err, @results) = @_;
    # Handle the results
  },
  'command1', 'arg1', 'arg2',
  { timeout => 10 }
);
```

In the above code, Mojo::IOLoop->subprocess is used to execute the command1 with arguments asynchronously in a separate process. The results are then handled in the provided callback.

Multi-threading:

While Mojo's event-driven model is based on a single-threaded event loop, you can still use Perl's multi-threading capabilities to perform concurrent tasks. You can utilize Perl's threads module to create and manage multiple threads, each executing a specific task concurrently.

```perl
use threads;

# Create and manage multiple threads
my @threads;
```

```perl
foreach my $task (@tasks) {
  push @threads, threads->create(\&task_function, $task);
}


# Wait for all threads to finish
$_->join foreach @threads;


sub task_function {
  my ($task) = @_;
  # Perform the task
}
```

In the above code, multiple threads are created, and each thread executes the task_function with a specific task.

It's important to note that when using parallel processing and multi-threading, you need to carefully handle synchronization, shared resources, and potential conflicts to ensure the correctness and stability of your application. Additionally, keep in mind that Mojo's event loop is not directly aware of parallel processing or multi-threading, so communication between different processes or threads may require additional considerations.

It's recommended to thoroughly test and benchmark your application when incorporating parallel processing and multi-threading to ensure optimal performance and stability.

SYNCHRONIZATION AND COMMUNICATION BETWEEN THREADS

When working with multi-threading in Mojo or any other Perl application, synchronization and communication between threads are crucial to ensure proper coordination and avoid data races or conflicts. Here are some techniques and tools you can use for synchronization and communication between threads:

Shared Variables:

To share data between threads, you can use shared variables provided by the threads::shared module. Shared variables ensure that data can be accessed and modified safely by multiple threads.

```perl
use threads;
use threads::shared;

# Create a shared variable
my $shared_data :shared;

# Modify shared data in threads
threads->create(sub {
    lock($shared_data);  # Lock the shared variable
    $shared_data = "Modified data";
```

```
});
```

```perl
# Access shared data in the main thread
lock($shared_data);  # Lock the shared variable
print $shared_data;
```

In the above code, $shared_data is a shared variable that can be safely accessed and modified by multiple threads. The lock function is used to lock the shared variable before accessing or modifying it to prevent data races.

Thread Synchronization Primitives:

Perl provides various synchronization primitives to coordinate the execution of threads and ensure proper synchronization. These include locks, conditions, semaphores, and barriers. You can use these primitives to control access to shared resources and synchronize the execution of threads.

```perl
use threads;
use threads::shared;

# Create a shared variable
my $shared_data :shared;

# Create a lock
my $lock :shared = 0;

# Modify shared data in threads using a lock
```

```perl
threads->create(sub {

    lock($lock);  # Acquire the lock

    $shared_data = "Modified data";

    unlock($lock);  # Release the lock

});
```

```perl
# Access shared data in the main thread using a lock

lock($lock);  # Acquire the lock

print $shared_data;

unlock($lock);  # Release the lock
```

In the above code, a lock is used to synchronize access to the shared variable $shared_data. The lock and unlock functions are used to acquire and release the lock, respectively.

Thread Signaling:

Thread signaling allows threads to notify each other about specific events or conditions. This can be achieved using condition variables provided by the threads::shared module. Condition variables allow threads to wait until a certain condition is met or to signal other threads to continue.

```perl
use threads;

use threads::shared;
```

```perl
# Create a shared condition variable

my $condition :shared = 0;
```

```perl
# Wait for the condition to be signaled in a thread
threads->create(sub {
    lock($condition);  # Acquire the lock associated with the condition variable
    cond_wait($condition);  # Wait for the condition to be signaled
    # Continue with further processing
});


# Signal the condition in the main thread
lock($condition);  # Acquire the lock associated with the condition variable
cond_signal($condition);  # Signal the condition
```

In the above code, a condition variable is used to synchronize the execution of threads. The cond_wait function is used to wait for the condition to be signaled, while the cond_signal function is used to signal the condition.

These are just a few examples of synchronization and communication techniques in multi-threaded Perl applications. It's important to carefully design and test your code to ensure proper synchronization and avoid potential issues such as deadlocks or race conditions. The threads module and threads::shared module provide more advanced features and methods for synchronization, and you can refer to their documentation for further information.

Dealing with common concurrency challenges

Concurrency introduces several challenges that need to be addressed when developing applications in Mojo. Here are some common challenges and strategies for dealing with them:

Race Conditions:

Race conditions occur when multiple threads or processes access and modify shared data simultaneously, leading to unpredictable results. To mitigate race conditions, you can use synchronization techniques such as locks, semaphores, or atomic operations to ensure that only one thread or process can access the shared data at a time. Proper synchronization ensures that data integrity is maintained and prevents race conditions.

Deadlocks:

Deadlocks occur when two or more threads or processes are waiting for each other to release resources, resulting in a stalemate where none of them can proceed. To avoid deadlocks, it's important to carefully design your synchronization mechanisms and ensure that locks are acquired and released in a consistent and proper order. Additionally, consider using timeout mechanisms or deadlock detection algorithms to handle exceptional cases where deadlocks might occur.

Starvation:

Starvation happens when a thread or process is perpetually denied access to a shared resource or is constantly preempted by other threads. This can lead to performance degradation and unfairness. To address starvation, you can implement fairness policies such as using a queue or priority system to ensure that all threads or processes get a fair chance to access shared resources. Additionally, you can consider using techniques like thread or process prioritization to allocate resources more evenly.

Resource Contention:

Resource contention occurs when multiple threads or processes compete for limited resources, resulting in performance bottlenecks. To mitigate resource contention, identify the critical sections of your code that access shared resources and minimize the time spent in those sections. Consider using fine-grained locking or other synchronization techniques to reduce the scope of contention. Additionally, optimizing algorithms and data structures can help alleviate resource contention and improve overall performance.

Thread Safety:

Ensuring thread safety is crucial when working with concurrent programming. Thread safety means that your code can be safely executed by multiple threads without causing data corruption or unexpected behavior. To achieve thread safety, use synchronization mechanisms, such as locks or atomic operations, to protect shared data from simultaneous access. Avoid global variables or shared mutable state when possible and favor immutable or thread-local data structures.

Debugging and Testing:

Debugging concurrent programs can be challenging due to their non-deterministic nature. Use debugging tools and techniques specifically designed for concurrent programs, such as thread analyzers or race condition detectors, to identify and resolve issues. Additionally, thorough testing with various input scenarios and load conditions can help uncover hidden concurrency bugs and validate the correctness of your application.

By addressing these challenges and employing appropriate concurrency management techniques, you can develop robust and efficient concurrent applications in Mojo. It's crucial to have a solid understanding of concurrent programming principles and to carefully design and test your code to ensure correct and reliable behavior in a multi-threaded or multi-process environment.

CHAPTER 8: ADVANCED MOJO TECHNIQUES

METAPROGRAMMING AND CODE GENERATION IN MOJO

Metaprogramming and code generation are powerful techniques in Mojo that allow you to dynamically generate and modify code at runtime. These techniques enable you to automate repetitive tasks, enhance code reusability, and create more flexible and efficient applications. Here's an overview of metaprogramming and code generation in Mojo:

Code Generation:

Code generation involves programmatically generating source code based on certain rules or templates. In Mojo, you can use code generation to create classes, methods, functions, or other code structures dynamically. This can be useful for generating boilerplate code, creating dynamic APIs, or building domain-specific languages (DSLs).

use Mojo::Base -strict;

sub generate_code {

   my ($class, $name, $attributes) = @_;

```perl
    my $code = <<"EOF";
package My::Class::$name;
use Mojo::Base -base;

has $_ => undef for qw(@$attributes);
EOF

    eval $code;
    die "Failed to generate code: $@" if $@;
}


# Generate a class dynamically
generate_code('My::Class', 'Person', ['name', 'age']);
```

In the above example, the generate_code function dynamically generates a class with specified attributes using a code template. The generated code is then evaluated using eval to create the class.

Metaprogramming:

Metaprogramming involves writing code that manipulates or extends the behavior of other code. In Mojo, metaprogramming is often achieved using features like introspection and dynamic method generation. You can use metaprogramming to modify classes, add methods, change inheritance, modify method behavior, and more.

```perl
use Mojo::Base -strict;

# Modify a class dynamically
my $class = 'My::Class::Person';
no strict 'refs';
push @{"${class}::ISA"}, 'My::Class::Human';

# Add a method dynamically
*{"${class}::greet"} = sub {
    my ($self) = @_;
    return "Hello, I am $self->{name}!";
};

# Create an object and call the dynamically added method
my $person = $class->new(name => 'John');
say $person->greet();
```

In the above code, the class My::Class::Person is modified dynamically by adding My::Class::Human as its parent class and adding a greet method to the class.

Template Toolkit:

Mojo integrates with Template Toolkit, a powerful templating system that allows you to generate code or text files based on templates. Template Toolkit provides a rich set of features for conditionals, loops, variable substitution, and more. You can use Template Toolkit to generate code files, HTML templates, configuration files, and other textual content.

```perl
use Mojo::Template;

# Load and render a template
my $template = Mojo::Template->new;
my $output = $template->render_file('template.tt', { name => 'John' });

# Generate a Perl module from a template
my $perl_code = $template->render(<<'EOF', { class => 'MyClass' });
package <%= $class %>;

sub new {
    my ($class, %args) = @_;
    ...
}
EOF
```

In the above example, a template file (template.tt) is loaded and rendered using Template Toolkit. Template variables can be substituted dynamically, and the rendered output can be stored in a variable or written to a file.

Metaprogramming and code generation in Mojo provide a lot of flexibility and can greatly simplify complex tasks. However, it's important to use these techniques judiciously and ensure proper testing and validation of the generated code. Be mindful of the impact on code readability, maintainability, and debugging when using metaprogramming techniques.

CREATING DOMAIN-SPECIFIC LANGUAGES (DSLs) WITH MOJO

Creating domain-specific languages (DSLs) with Mojo can be a powerful approach to build expressive and intuitive interfaces tailored to specific problem domains. DSLs allow you to define a language that is specifically designed to address the needs of a particular domain, making it easier for developers to write code in a more natural and concise manner. Here's an overview of how you can create DSLs with Mojo:

Define DSL Syntax:

Start by defining the syntax and structure of your DSL. Consider the specific tasks or concepts you want to express in a more domain-specific way. Determine the keywords, operators, and constructs that will make your DSL expressive and intuitive for its intended users.

Implement DSL Parser:

Create a parser that can understand and interpret the DSL syntax. Mojo provides a range of tools for parsing and processing input, including regular expressions, pattern matching, and built-in parsers like Mojo::DOM or Mojo::JSON. You can also leverage external parser generators, such as Parse::RecDescent or Marpa::R2, for more complex DSLs.

Define DSL Semantics:

Once the DSL syntax is parsed, define the semantics or meaning behind the DSL constructs. Determine how each DSL statement or construct should be executed and what actions should be taken. This may involve calling existing Mojo methods, invoking custom logic, or interacting with external systems.

Implement DSL API:

Create a set of functions, methods, or classes that serve as the API for your DSL. These functions should provide an interface to interact with the DSL and execute the desired actions. It's important to design the API in a way that aligns with the language constructs and idioms of the DSL, making it intuitive and easy to use.

Provide DSL Documentation:

Document your DSL thoroughly to guide users on how to write code using the DSL syntax and API. Explain the purpose and usage of each DSL construct, provide examples, and document any restrictions or limitations. Clear and comprehensive documentation helps users understand and leverage the DSL effectively.

Example DSL Usage:

Here's a simple example to illustrate how you can create a DSL for defining routes in Mojo:

```perl
package MyApp::Routes;

use Mojo::Base -base;
use Mojo::Util qw(slurp);
use Mojo::JSON qw(decode_json);

has 'routes' => sub { [] };

sub get {
   my ($self, $path, $handler) = @_;
   push @{$self->routes}, { method => 'GET', path => $path, handler => $handler };
}

sub post {
   my ($self, $path, $handler) = @_;
   push @{$self->routes}, { method => 'POST', path => $path, handler => $handler };
}
```

```perl
sub load_from_file {

    my ($self, $file) = @_;

    my $dsl_code = slurp($file);

    my $dsl_data = decode_json($dsl_code);


    for my $route (@{$dsl_data->{routes}}) {

        $self->$route->{method}($route->{path}, $route->{handler});

    }

}
```

In the example above, we define a DSL for defining routes. The DSL provides get and post methods that allow users to define routes using a more intuitive and concise syntax. The load_from_file method demonstrates how the DSL can be loaded from a file and executed to define routes.

By creating a DSL, you can enhance the readability and maintainability of your code, as well as improve the developer experience when working within a specific domain. It's important to strike a balance between expressiveness and complexity, ensuring that the DSL remains easy to understand and use for its intended audience.

Debugging and optimizing Mojo code

Debugging and optimizing Mojo code are important steps in ensuring the reliability and efficiency of your applications. Here are some techniques and tools you can use for debugging and optimizing your Mojo code:

Debugging Techniques:

Use say, say STDERR, or warn statements to print debugging information to the console or error log. This can help you understand the flow of your code and identify any issues or unexpected behavior.

Utilize Mojo's logging capabilities by using methods such as app->log->debug or app->log->error to output log messages at different levels of severity. This allows you to track the execution flow and monitor the application's behavior.

Enable debugging mode ($app->mode('development')) to get detailed error messages and stack traces when exceptions occur. This is particularly useful during development and debugging stages.

Use the Mojo Debugger module (Mojo::Debug) to step through your code, set breakpoints, and inspect variables. It provides a convenient interactive debugging environment within your Mojo application.

Profiling and Performance Optimization:

Use the built-in Mojo profiler (Mojo::UserAgent::Transactor::Base) to identify performance bottlenecks in your code. It allows you to measure the execution time of various parts of your application and identify areas that require optimization.

Leverage tools like Devel::NYTProf or Dancer::Plugin::NYTProf to perform detailed code profiling. These tools can help you identify hotspots in your code and pinpoint areas that consume excessive time or resources.

Optimize database interactions by using appropriate indexing, optimizing queries, and leveraging caching mechanisms.

Identify and optimize resource-intensive operations such as file I/O, network communication, or computationally expensive tasks. Consider using asynchronous or non-blocking techniques (e.g., Mojo::IOLoop) to improve overall performance.

Use Mojo's caching mechanisms, such as Mojo::Cache, to store frequently accessed data in memory and reduce the need for repetitive computations or expensive operations.

Testing and Quality Assurance:

Implement comprehensive unit tests using a testing framework like Test::Mojo or Test::More to ensure the correctness of your code and catch issues early on.

Use code coverage tools like Devel::Cover or Test::Coverage to identify areas of your code that are not adequately covered by tests. This helps you ensure that your tests exercise all parts of your codebase.

Consider using code quality tools like Perl::Critic or Mojolicious::Plugin::Lint to enforce coding standards, improve readability, and detect potential issues.

Monitoring and Logging:

Implement monitoring and logging solutions to collect and analyze runtime information about your Mojo application. This can include metrics such as response times, error rates, memory usage, and other performance indicators. Tools like Prometheus and Grafana can help in visualizing and analyzing this data.

Remember to focus your optimization efforts on areas that have the most significant impact on performance and user experience. It's essential to measure the performance before and after applying optimizations to validate their effectiveness.

By employing these techniques, you can identify and resolve issues, improve the performance of your Mojo applications, and ensure a smooth and efficient user experience.

Exploring advanced libraries and frameworks in Mojo

Mojo provides a rich ecosystem of advanced libraries and frameworks that can enhance your development process and expand the capabilities of your Mojo applications. Here are some notable libraries and frameworks worth exploring:

Mojolicious Plugins:

Mojolicious::Plugin::Authentication: Provides authentication capabilities for your application, including various authentication methods like OAuth, OpenID, and database-based authentication.

Mojolicious::Plugin::Database: Simplifies database connectivity and interaction by providing an intuitive API for working with databases, including support for different database backends.

Mojolicious::Plugin::WebSocket: Adds WebSocket support to your Mojo application, allowing real-time bidirectional communication between clients and servers.

Web Application Frameworks:

Dancer2: A lightweight and flexible web application framework inspired by Mojo. It offers an expressive syntax and supports various plugins for authentication, database connectivity, and more.

Catalyst: A powerful and extensible web application framework that provides advanced features such as MVC architecture, caching, session management, and more.

Templating Engines:

Template Toolkit: A versatile and feature-rich templating engine that allows you to separate the presentation logic from your application code. It provides a wide range of features like conditionals, loops, filters, and macros.

Text::Xslate: A fast and powerful templating engine that supports multiple template syntaxes, including Template Toolkit, and provides a flexible and efficient template rendering solution.

Testing Frameworks:

Test::Mojo: A testing framework specifically designed for Mojo applications. It provides convenient methods for simulating requests, handling responses, and making assertions about the behavior of your application.

Test::More: A popular testing framework in the Perl ecosystem that provides a rich set of testing functions and assertions for writing comprehensive unit tests.

Data Manipulation Libraries:

Mojo::JSON: Provides JSON parsing and generation capabilities. It allows you to encode and decode JSON data and interact with JSON-based APIs.

Mojo::DOM: A powerful library for parsing and manipulating HTML/XML documents. It enables you to extract data, traverse the document structure, and perform various DOM operations.

Asynchronous Programming:

Mojo::IOLoop: A robust and efficient event loop implementation for building high-performance, non-blocking applications. It provides a wide range of functionalities for handling I/O operations, timers, and callbacks in an asynchronous manner.

Promises: Mojo supports Promises-based programming using modules like Mojo::Promise and Mojo::Promise::Role. Promises allow you to write asynchronous code in a more structured and readable way, handling complex control flows and chaining operations.

RESTful API Development:

Mojolicious::Plugin::Swagger2: Enables the generation of RESTful APIs based on Swagger/OpenAPI specifications. It simplifies the process of creating and documenting APIs with automatic route generation and input/output validation.

These are just a few examples of the advanced libraries and frameworks available in the Mojo ecosystem. You can explore the Mojolicious website (https://mojolicious.org/) and the CPAN (Comprehensive Perl Archive Network) to discover more libraries and frameworks that can enhance your Mojo development experience and extend the capabilities of your applications.

CHAPTER 9: MOJO AND THE INTERNET OF THINGS (IOT)

INTRODUCTION TO IoT AND ITS SIGNIFICANCE

IoT, or the Internet of Things, refers to the network of interconnected physical devices, vehicles, appliances, and other objects embedded with sensors, software, and connectivity capabilities that enable them to collect and exchange data. These devices communicate with each other and with central systems over the internet, creating a vast network of interconnected "things."

The significance of IoT lies in its potential to revolutionize various aspects of our lives, industries, and societies. Here are some key points highlighting the significance of IoT:

Connectivity and Data Collection: IoT enables devices to connect and communicate with each other, collecting and exchanging data in real-time. This data can be leveraged to gain valuable insights, improve decision-making, and optimize operations. For example, in industrial settings, IoT devices can collect data on machine performance, energy usage, and production metrics, allowing businesses to make data-driven decisions for process optimization.

Automation and Efficiency: IoT can automate various processes, reducing human intervention and increasing efficiency. Smart home devices, for instance, can control lighting, heating, and security systems based on predefined rules or user preferences. In manufacturing, IoT-enabled automation can optimize production lines, monitor equipment health, and enable predictive maintenance, leading to improved productivity and reduced downtime.

Enhanced Safety and Security: IoT can improve safety and security across different domains. For instance, smart surveillance systems equipped with IoT devices can monitor public spaces, detect anomalies, and respond to potential threats in real-time. In healthcare, IoT devices can track patient vitals, monitor medication adherence, and alert healthcare providers in case of emergencies.

Smart Cities and Infrastructure: IoT plays a vital role in the development of smart cities, where interconnected devices and systems enable efficient resource management, traffic optimization, waste management, and energy conservation. By integrating IoT technologies into infrastructure, cities can enhance sustainability, improve quality of life, and reduce costs.

Improved Healthcare and Well-being: IoT devices have the potential to transform healthcare by enabling remote patient monitoring, personalized medicine, and telehealth services. Connected medical devices can collect patient data, transmit it to healthcare providers, and facilitate timely interventions. IoT can also promote healthy lifestyles by monitoring fitness activities, sleep patterns, and nutrition, providing individuals with actionable insights for well-being.

Environmental Impact: IoT can contribute to environmental conservation and sustainability efforts. Connected sensors and monitoring devices can measure air quality, water quality, and energy consumption, helping identify areas for improvement and supporting sustainable practices. For example, smart grids can optimize energy distribution and reduce waste, while precision agriculture techniques can optimize water usage and improve crop yield.

Overall, IoT's significance lies in its ability to connect and empower various devices, systems, and industries, enabling data-driven insights, automation, and improved efficiency. It has the potential to transform how we live, work, and interact with the world, offering numerous opportunities for innovation and positive societal impact.

BUILDING IOT APPLICATIONS WITH MOJO

Building IoT applications with Mojo can be a powerful combination, as Mojo provides a robust framework for web development and handling asynchronous tasks, while IoT involves connecting and interacting with physical devices. Here are some steps to get started with building IoT applications using Mojo:

Identify the IoT Use Case: Determine the specific IoT use case or application you want to build. This could be anything from home automation, industrial monitoring, smart agriculture, or healthcare applications. Define the goals and requirements of your application, including the devices you want to connect, the data you want to collect, and the actions you want to perform.

Select IoT Hardware and Protocols: Choose the IoT hardware and communication protocols that align with your use case. This could include sensors, actuators, microcontrollers, or development boards such as Arduino or Raspberry Pi. Identify the communication protocols (e.g., MQTT, HTTP, WebSocket) that will be used for device-to-device or device-to-server communication.

Set Up the Mojo Development Environment: Install Mojo and set up your development environment. Refer to the Mojo documentation (https://mojolicious.org/) for installation instructions and guidelines. Ensure that you have a working Perl installation and all required dependencies.

Design the Web Application: Determine the web application's architecture and design. Identify the key features and functionalities of your IoT application, such as data visualization, device management, real-time monitoring, and control interfaces. Utilize Mojo's MVC architecture to structure your application and separate concerns.

Implement Device Communication: Use Mojo's powerful networking capabilities to establish communication between your web application and IoT devices. Depending on the chosen communication protocol, you may need to implement client-side code in Mojo to send/receive data from devices and server-side code to handle incoming device data.

Handle Asynchronous Operations: As IoT applications involve real-time data collection and interactions, utilize Mojo's asynchronous capabilities to handle concurrent operations. Use Mojo::IOLoop to manage event-driven programming, handle non-blocking I/O operations, and efficiently process multiple requests simultaneously.

Implement Data Storage and Retrieval: Decide on the data storage approach for your IoT application. This could involve using databases, file systems, or cloud-based storage services to store and retrieve device data. Mojo provides support for interacting with various databases, such as SQLite, MySQL, and PostgreSQL, allowing you to seamlessly integrate data storage capabilities.

Implement Real-Time Updates and Notifications: Utilize Mojo's WebSocket capabilities to enable real-time updates and notifications in your IoT application. WebSocket communication allows for bi-directional communication between the server and clients, enabling real-time data streaming and instant updates on device statuses or alerts.

Implement Security Measures: Ensure the security of your IoT application by implementing appropriate security measures. This may include authentication and authorization mechanisms, data encryption, secure communication protocols, and access control to protect sensitive data and prevent unauthorized access.

Test and Deploy: Test your IoT application thoroughly to ensure its functionality, reliability, and performance. Write unit tests using testing frameworks like Test::Mojo to verify the behavior of your application's components. Once you are confident in your application, deploy it to a production environment or the target platform.

Remember to iterate and continuously improve your IoT application based on user feedback, emerging technologies, and evolving requirements. The Mojo framework provides flexibility, scalability, and a wide range of tools and libraries to help you build robust and feature-rich IoT applications.

INTERACTING WITH SENSORS, ACTUATORS, AND IOT DEVICES

Interacting with sensors, actuators, and IoT devices is a crucial aspect of building IoT applications. Here are some guidelines on how to interact with these devices using Mojo:

Identify Device APIs and Protocols: Determine the APIs and protocols supported by the sensors, actuators, or IoT devices you are using. Common protocols include MQTT, HTTP, CoAP, and WebSocket. This information will help you establish communication between your Mojo application and the devices.

Establish Device Connections: Use Mojo's networking capabilities to establish connections with the devices. Depending on the chosen protocol, you may need to implement client-side code to connect to the devices and send/receive data. Mojo provides modules like Mojo::UserAgent and Mojo::WebSocket to handle HTTP and WebSocket communication, respectively.

Handle Sensor Data: Read sensor data from the connected devices using the appropriate APIs or protocols. Parse and process the incoming data in your Mojo application to extract the required information. You can use Mojo's JSON or XML handling capabilities to parse data received from the devices.

Control Actuators: To control actuators or send commands to IoT devices, use the corresponding APIs or protocols supported by the devices. This could involve sending HTTP requests, publishing messages to a message broker using MQTT, or using other device-specific communication methods. Implement the necessary logic in your Mojo application to send commands or control the actuators based on user input or application logic.

Implement Event-Driven Logic: Leverage Mojo's event-driven programming model to handle incoming sensor data or device events. Use Mojo::IOLoop and event handlers to process incoming data asynchronously, trigger actions based on sensor readings, or respond to device events. This allows your application to operate efficiently and respond to real-time updates from the devices.

Error Handling and Resilience: Implement error handling mechanisms in your Mojo application to handle device communication failures, network disruptions, or unexpected sensor readings. Handle exceptions, timeouts, and error conditions gracefully to ensure the stability and reliability of your application. Implement reconnection strategies or fallback mechanisms to recover from temporary communication failures.

Security Considerations: Ensure that proper security measures are in place when interacting with IoT devices. This may include authentication, encryption, and secure communication protocols to protect sensitive data and prevent unauthorized access to the devices. Implement secure practices and follow best practices for IoT device communication to maintain the integrity and confidentiality of the data.

Testing and Debugging: Test your device interaction code thoroughly to ensure it functions as expected. Write unit tests using testing frameworks like Test::Mojo to verify the behavior of your device interaction logic. Utilize debugging techniques and tools, such as logging and printing debug information, to troubleshoot issues and ensure proper communication with the devices.

Remember to refer to the documentation and specifications provided by the sensor, actuator, or IoT device manufacturers for guidance on their specific APIs, protocols, and communication requirements. Adhere to their recommended practices and guidelines to ensure optimal interaction with the devices.

INTEGRATING CLOUD SERVICES AND MQTT IN MOJO-BASED IOT PROJECTS

Integrating cloud services and MQTT in Mojo-based IoT projects can enhance the scalability, data storage, and real-time communication capabilities of your application. Here's how you can accomplish this:

Choose a Cloud Service Provider: Select a cloud service provider that supports MQTT, such as Amazon Web Services (AWS) IoT Core, Google Cloud IoT Core, or Microsoft Azure IoT Hub. These platforms provide managed MQTT brokers and a range of services for IoT data ingestion, storage, and processing.

Set Up MQTT Connectivity: Establish MQTT connectivity between your Mojo application and the cloud MQTT broker. Utilize Mojo's networking capabilities to connect to the MQTT broker using the appropriate protocol (typically MQTT or MQTT over WebSocket). Mojo::UserAgent and Mojo::WebSocket can be used to handle the MQTT connection.

Publish Data to the MQTT Broker: Use Mojo's MQTT client libraries or modules (e.g., Net::MQTT::Simple) to publish data from your Mojo application to the MQTT broker. Convert the data from your IoT devices into the desired MQTT payload format (e.g., JSON) and publish it to the relevant MQTT topic(s) associated with your cloud service.

Subscribe to MQTT Topics: Subscribe to MQTT topics on the cloud MQTT broker to receive incoming messages or commands from the cloud service. Implement appropriate event handlers in your Mojo application to process the incoming MQTT messages and trigger actions based on the received data or commands.

Implement Cloud Service Integration: Integrate your Mojo application with the cloud service APIs provided by the chosen cloud platform. This may involve sending data to cloud storage services, invoking cloud functions or serverless compute, or leveraging cloud analytics and machine learning services for data processing and insights generation.

Handle Authentication and Security: Ensure that proper authentication and security measures are in place when interacting with the cloud service. This may include using authentication tokens, TLS encryption for secure communication, and implementing access control mechanisms to restrict access to your cloud resources.

Data Storage and Retrieval: Leverage the cloud service's data storage capabilities to store and retrieve IoT data. Cloud providers often offer scalable databases, data lakes, or time-series databases for efficient storage and querying of large volumes of IoT data. Utilize Mojo's database integration modules (e.g., Mojo::SQLite, Mojo::Pg) to interact with the cloud databases.

Real-Time Communication: Leverage MQTT's pub/sub pattern and Mojo's WebSocket capabilities to establish real-time bidirectional communication between your Mojo application and the cloud service. Use MQTT for publishing and subscribing to real-time data updates, and WebSocket for handling real-time notifications and bidirectional communication.

Data Analytics and Insights: Explore cloud service features for data analytics and insights generation. Many cloud platforms provide tools and services for processing, analyzing, and visualizing IoT data, allowing you to gain actionable insights from your IoT application's data streams.

Monitor and Scale: Utilize the monitoring and scaling capabilities offered by the cloud service to ensure the reliability and scalability of your Mojo-based IoT application. Monitor the performance, health, and usage metrics of your application and leverage the auto-scaling features of the cloud platform to handle increased load or demand.

By integrating cloud services and MQTT into your Mojo-based IoT projects, you can leverage the scalability, data processing, and real-time communication capabilities of cloud platforms to enhance the functionality and performance of your application.

CHAPTER 10: FUTURE OF MOJO AND BEYOND

CURRENT TRENDS AND FUTURE PROSPECTS OF MOJO

Increased Adoption of Mojo: Mojo has gained popularity as a powerful and flexible web framework within the Perl community. Its ease of use, robustness, and extensive feature set have attracted developers to build web applications, APIs, and IoT solutions using Mojo. The continued adoption of Mojo is expected as more developers recognize its benefits and leverage its capabilities.

Emphasis on Asynchronous and Non-Blocking IO: Mojo's strength lies in its asynchronous and non-blocking IO capabilities, allowing developers to handle concurrent operations efficiently. This aligns with the growing need for high-performance applications that can handle numerous concurrent requests, making Mojo well-suited for building real-time applications, IoT solutions, and APIs.

Integration with Modern Web Technologies: Mojo continues to evolve and integrate with modern web technologies to stay relevant and meet the demands of modern web development. It embraces trends like RESTful APIs, WebSockets, and JSON, enabling developers to build responsive and interactive web applications.

Support for Microservices Architecture: Microservices architecture is gaining popularity for building scalable and modular applications. Mojo's lightweight and modular nature make it a suitable framework for developing microservices-based applications. The ability to build and manage individual components as separate Mojo applications allows for easier scalability and maintainability.

Continued Community Support and Development: The Mojo community remains active and supportive, providing continuous development, updates, and bug fixes. The framework has an extensive set of plugins, libraries, and modules contributed by the community, expanding the functionality and capabilities of Mojo.

Expansion in IoT and Real-time Applications: Mojo's asynchronous nature and support for WebSockets make it well-suited for building IoT applications and real-time communication systems. As the IoT industry continues to grow and real-time applications become more prevalent, Mojo's capabilities in handling asynchronous tasks and real-time data processing could position it as a favorable choice for these domains.

Integration with AI and Machine Learning: With the increasing demand for AI and machine learning applications, integrating Mojo with AI frameworks and libraries can open up new possibilities. Developers may explore leveraging Mojo's capabilities for building AI-powered web applications, chatbots, data processing pipelines, or integrating AI models into existing Mojo-based systems.

It's important to note that technology trends and the future direction of Mojo may evolve over time based on the preferences of developers, emerging technologies, and industry demands. To stay up to date with the latest trends and developments, it's recommended to follow the official Mojo documentation, community forums, and keep an eye on relevant technology news and updates.

Community and resources for Mojo developers

The Mojo community is active and supportive, providing several resources for developers to learn, collaborate, and get assistance. Here are some valuable community and resources for Mojo developers:

Official Documentation: The official Mojo website (https://mojolicious.org/) provides comprehensive documentation, including guides, tutorials, API references, and examples. It covers all aspects of Mojo, from installation and basic usage to advanced topics like web development, testing, and deployment.

Community Forums: The Mojolicious community maintains a discussion forum called "Mojolicious::Plugin::Mojolicious" on Google Groups (https://groups.google.com/g/mojolicious) where developers can ask questions, seek help, and participate in discussions related to Mojo development. It's an excellent platform to interact with other Mojo developers, share knowledge, and learn from experienced members.

GitHub Repository: The Mojo project is hosted on GitHub (https://github.com/mojolicious/mojo), providing access to the source code, issue tracker, and a vibrant community of contributors. Developers can contribute to the project, report issues, and explore the codebase to gain insights into the internals of Mojo.

Mojo Plugins and Modules: The Mojo ecosystem offers a wide range of plugins and modules contributed by the community. These extensions provide additional functionality, such as database integration, authentication, template engines, and much more. The Mojolicious Plugins organization on GitHub (https://github.com/mojolicious-plugins) hosts many popular plugins that can be utilized in Mojo projects.

Mojocasts: Mojocasts (https://mojocasts.com/) is a website that offers video tutorials and screencasts covering various aspects of Mojo development. It provides step-by-step guidance on different topics, including web development, testing, and advanced features of Mojo.

CPAN: The Comprehensive Perl Archive Network (CPAN) (https://metacpan.org/) is a vast repository of Perl modules. It hosts numerous Mojo-related modules, including Mojo-specific libraries, utilities, and tools. Developers can search CPAN for Mojo-related modules and leverage them to enhance their Mojo projects.

IRC Channel: The Mojolicious community maintains an IRC channel (#mojo) on the irc.libera.chat network. It serves as a live chat platform where developers can engage in real-time discussions, ask questions, and get help from experienced Mojo developers.

Conferences and Meetups: Perl and Mojo-related conferences and meetups provide opportunities to connect with fellow developers, learn from experts, and stay updated with the latest trends. Keep an eye on Perl-related events and consider attending those that focus on Mojo or web development to expand your network and knowledge.

Blogs and Online Resources: Several developers and contributors in the Mojo community share their experiences, tutorials, and insights through personal blogs and online resources. Searching for Mojo-related topics on search engines can lead you to informative blog posts, articles, and tutorials written by experienced Mojo developers.

By utilizing these community resources, developers can gain knowledge, find answers to their questions, stay up to date with the latest developments, and connect with fellow Mojo enthusiasts. Active participation in the community can foster learning, collaboration, and growth in Mojo development.

Exploring real-world applications of Mojo

Mojo is a versatile web framework with a wide range of applications. Here are some examples of real-world applications where Mojo has been utilized:

Web Applications: Mojo is commonly used for building web applications of various sizes and complexities. It provides features like routing, templating, session management, and form handling that facilitate the development of dynamic and interactive web interfaces. Mojo's asynchronous nature and event-driven architecture make it suitable for creating real-time web applications, chat systems, and collaborative platforms.

APIs and Microservices: Mojo's lightweight and modular design make it well-suited for developing APIs and microservices. It allows developers to define API endpoints, handle JSON or XML request/response formats, and integrate with external services using Mojo's client modules. Mojo's asynchronous capabilities enable efficient handling of concurrent API requests and non-blocking IO operations.

Internet of Things (IoT) Solutions: Mojo's non-blocking IO and event-driven architecture make it suitable for building IoT applications. It can handle real-time data streaming from IoT devices, communicate with MQTT brokers, and interact with sensors and actuators. Mojo's ability to handle asynchronous tasks, websockets, and event-driven programming is beneficial for building IoT dashboards, data processing pipelines, and real-time monitoring systems.

Command-line Tools: Mojo can be used to build command-line tools and utilities. It provides a robust foundation for creating scripts that automate tasks, process data, and interact with external services via APIs. Mojo's features like command-line argument parsing, output formatting, and integration with external libraries make it useful for building command-line interfaces (CLIs) with rich functionality.

Testing and Development Tools: Mojo includes testing utilities and modules that facilitate automated testing of web applications and APIs. Developers can write unit tests and integration tests using frameworks like Test::Mojo, enabling them to ensure the quality and stability of their Mojo-based applications. Mojo's built-in development server and interactive REPL (Read-Eval-Print Loop) also aid in rapid prototyping and testing during the development phase.

Web Scraping and Data Extraction: Mojo's HTML/XML parsing capabilities, DOM traversal, and CSS selector-based querying make it an excellent choice for web scraping and data extraction tasks. Developers can write Mojo scripts to crawl websites, extract specific data elements, and process the collected data for analysis or integration into other systems.

Prototyping and Proof of Concepts: Mojo's simplicity and rapid development capabilities make it ideal for prototyping and proof of concept (POC) projects. It enables developers to quickly build functional prototypes to demonstrate ideas, showcase features, and validate concepts before investing further resources in development.

These are just a few examples of the diverse applications where Mojo has been successfully utilized. Due to its flexibility, asynchronous capabilities, and extensive feature set, Mojo can be applied in various domains, ranging from web development to IoT, automation, and data processing. Developers continue to explore and leverage Mojo's strengths to build innovative and efficient solutions in different industries and use cases.

What lies ahead: Exciting possibilities with Mojo

While the future of Mojo and its possibilities are determined by the direction of its development and the needs of its user community, there are several exciting possibilities that lie ahead:

Continued Framework Enhancements: Mojo is an actively maintained framework, and its development team is dedicated to improving and expanding its capabilities. This includes introducing new features, enhancing existing functionality, and addressing performance and security considerations. Future updates may introduce innovative concepts, integrations with emerging technologies, and improvements in developer productivity.

Integration with Modern Web Technologies: Mojo is likely to continue integrating with modern web technologies to stay relevant and meet the demands of modern web development. This may include deeper integration with JavaScript frameworks, enhanced support for client-side frameworks, and improved interoperability with frontend technologies like React, Angular, or Vue.js. Such integrations would allow developers to leverage the best of both worlds and build more powerful and interactive web applications.

Advances in Asynchronous Programming: Mojo's asynchronous and non-blocking IO capabilities provide high performance and scalability. As asynchronous programming becomes even more prevalent in modern software development, Mojo may further evolve to provide more advanced tools, patterns, and optimizations for handling concurrent operations, making it even more efficient for building real-time applications, IoT systems, and highly concurrent server-side applications.

Increased IoT and Edge Computing Integration: The growth of the Internet of Things (IoT) and edge computing presents exciting opportunities for Mojo. Mojo's lightweight nature, non-blocking IO, and support for IoT protocols like MQTT position it well for developing IoT solutions. Future advancements in Mojo may include improved support for IoT device management, edge computing architectures, and integrations with cloud platforms designed for IoT and edge computing use cases.

Machine Learning and Artificial Intelligence: With the increasing demand for AI and machine learning applications, Mojo could potentially integrate with AI and ML frameworks, making it easier for developers to build AI-powered web applications, chatbots, data processing pipelines, and other intelligent systems. Mojo's extensibility and flexibility may allow for seamless integration with popular AI and ML libraries, enabling developers to leverage AI capabilities within Mojo-based projects.

Community Contributions and Ecosystem Growth: Mojo's success and potential lie in the strength of its community. As more developers adopt Mojo and contribute plugins, modules, and libraries, the ecosystem will continue to grow and become more diverse. This will provide developers with a wider range of tools, integrations, and resources, further enhancing the capabilities and possibilities of Mojo.

It's important to note that these possibilities are speculative, and the actual direction of Mojo's development will be determined by the needs of its user community and the evolving technology landscape. Developers and enthusiasts are encouraged to actively participate in the Mojo community, share their ideas, contribute to the framework, and shape its future direction.

CONCLUSION

In conclusion, Mojo is a powerful and versatile web framework built on top of Perl that offers a range of features and capabilities for building web applications, APIs, IoT solutions, and more. Its asynchronous and non-blocking IO model, event-driven architecture, and extensive toolset make it a flexible and efficient framework for modern web development.

Throughout this book, we have explored various aspects of Mojo, starting from its introduction, history, and design philosophy. We delved into its syntax, data types, control flow, and functions, understanding how to build modular and well-organized code. We explored advanced concepts such as object-oriented programming, metaprogramming, and concurrent programming, enabling developers to take full advantage of Mojo's capabilities.

We also discussed the wide array of resources available for Mojo developers, including the official documentation, community forums, plugins, modules, and tutorials. These resources provide ample support for learning, troubleshooting, and collaborating with fellow developers.

Moreover, we explored real-world applications of Mojo, ranging from web applications and APIs to IoT solutions, command-line tools, and data extraction tasks. Mojo's versatility and adaptability make it suitable for a wide range of use cases.

Looking to the future, we discussed exciting possibilities for Mojo, including continued framework enhancements, integration with modern web technologies, IoT and edge computing integration, advancements in asynchronous programming, AI and ML integration, and the growth of the Mojo community and ecosystem.

Overall, Mojo offers developers a robust and efficient framework for building web applications and other software solutions. By leveraging its features, developers can create scalable, high-performance applications and stay at the forefront of modern web development. Whether you are a beginner or an experienced developer, Mojo provides a powerful toolkit to bring your ideas to life and develop innovative solutions in the ever-evolving world of technology.

THANK YOU!!

Made in the USA
Columbia, SC
09 April 2024